Why Why Why do bees make honey?

MiLeS KeLLy

PUBLISHING

First published in 2007 by
Miles Kelly Publishing Ltd
Bardfield Centre, Great Bardfield, Essex, CM7 4SL

Copyright © Miles Kelly Publishing Ltd 2007

2 4 6 8 10 9 7 5 3 1

Editorial Director
Belinda Gallagher

Art Director
Jo Brewer

Assistant Editor
Lucy Dowling

Volume Designer
Debbie Oatley

Indexer
Hilary Bird

Production Manager
Elizabeth Brunwin

Reprographics
Anthony Cambray, Liberty Newton, Ian Paulyn

ISBN 978-1-84236-906-7

Printed in China

British Library Cataloguing-in-Publication Data
A catalogue record for this book is available
from the British Library

www.mileskelly.net
info@mileskelly.net

Contents

Are all bugs insects?

Insects are the largest of all the animal groups. There are millions of different kinds that live almost everywhere in the world. Not all bugs are insects. Spiders belong to a group called arachnids, and millipedes are in yet another group called myriapods.

Garden spider is an arachnid

Pill millipede is a myriapod

Ladybird is an insect

Dinner date!

Breeding time is very dangerous for the praying mantis. After mating, the female may eat the male.

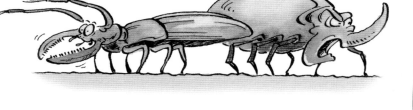

How many wings does an insect have?

Most insects have two pairs of wings and they use them to fly from place to place. A large moth flaps its wings once or twice each second, whilst some tiny flies flap their wings almost 1000 times each second.

Do insects have skeletons?

Insects do not have a bony skeleton inside their bodies like we do. Instead, their bodies are covered by a series of horny plates. This is called an exoskeleton.

Moth

Look

Have a look in your garden, under rocks and in the soil. How many different insects can you find?

Where do butterflies come from?

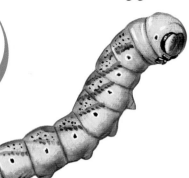

① Caterpillar hatches from an egg

Butterflies start off life as caterpillars – wriggly grubs that hatch from eggs. Caterpillars eat lots of leaves, and when they are big enough, they attach themselves to twigs. They form hard shells called pupas. Inside the pupa, the caterpillar changes into a butterfly. When the butterfly is fully formed, it breaks out of its pupa.

② Pupa is formed

③ Butterfly breaks out of its pupa

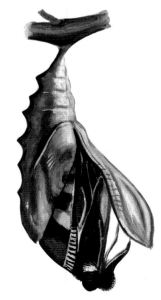

Fast mover!

The green tiger beetle is a fast-moving hunter that races over open ground. It chases smaller creatures such as ants, woodlice, worms and spiders.

④ Butterfly flies away

Peacock butterfly

Paint

Fold some paper in half. Open it up and paint two butterfly wings on one side. Fold it again and open it up to see all of the butterfly.

How far can a flea jump?

Fleas can jump a very long distance for their body size. These tiny insects measure just 2 to 3 millimetres in length. They can jump over 30 centimetres, which is more than 100 times their body size.

Flea

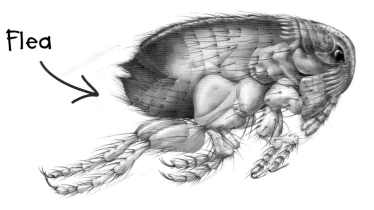

Which butterfly flies the highest?

One of the strongest insect fliers is the Apollo butterfly. It can fly high over hills and even mountains, then it rests on a rock or flower in the sunshine.

Why are butterflies brightly coloured?

Like many butterflies, the monarch butterfly has bright, bold colours on its wings. These warn other animals, such as birds and lizards, that it tastes horrible and is not good for them to eat.

Tasty treats!

Animal droppings are delicious to many kinds of insects. Various beetles lay their eggs in dung. The young insects then hatch out and eat it.

Where do cockroaches live?

Just about everywhere! Cockroaches are beetles that run quickly across the ground. They have low, flat bodies and can dart into small spaces under logs, stones and bricks. They can also hide in cupboards, furniture — and beds!

Cockroach

Monarch butterfly

Think

Write a list of any fast-running animals that you can think of.

Can insects walk on water?

Some insects can. The pondskater has a slim, light body with long, wide legs, which allow it to glide across the surface of the water.

Why do bees make honey?

Bees make sweet, sticky honey packed with energy. Wild bees make honey to feed themselves and their growing young, which are called larvae. Lots of animals eat honey, including humans, who keep honeybees in nests called hives so that the honey is easier to collect.

Honeybees

How many times can a bee sting you?

A bee can only sting once in its whole lifetime. After a bee jabs its sting into an enemy, the sting stays in its victim. As the bee flies away, the rear part of its body tears off and the bee soon dies.

Sting

Yummy!

Ants get food from insects called aphids. When an ant strokes an aphid, it oozes a drop of 'milk' called honeydew, which the ant then drinks.

Taste

Ask an adult if you can taste some honey. See if you think it tastes sweet and sticky, too.

Why do bees have a queen?

The queen bee lays all of the eggs, from which young bees hatch. Without her, there would be no other bees. Worker bees look after the queen and the eggs.

Why do spiders make silk?

Spiders make very thin, fine threads called silk. Some spiders use their silk to make webs to catch their prey. Other spiders wrap up their victims in silk to stop them escaping. Female spiders make silk bags called cocoons and lay their eggs in them.

Can spiders spit?

The spitting spider can. It feeds on mosquitoes, moths and flies. When it spots its prey, it spits a sticky silk thread over it. This stops the victim moving, so the spider can eat it.

fly stuck in web

Find

See if you can find a spider's web. Look in the corners of windows, in garages and in sheds.

12

Spider on its web

Do spiders have fangs?

Spiders have sharp fangs in their jaws, which they use to grab and bite their prey. The fangs inject a poison to kill the victim. The spider then eats its food by sucking out the body juices.

Crowded house!

A wasps' nest may have about 2000 wasps in it, but a termite colony may have over five million termites.

Why do crickets chirp?

Cricket

Male crickets chirp to attract the attention of female crickets. Their wings have hard, ridged strips at the base like a row of pegs, which make a chirping sound when they are rubbed together.

Pretend

Make your own insect noise and pretend to be an insect. Can you chirp like a cricket?

What is a termite?

Termites are small insects that are similar to ants. They live in large groups called colonies, which include king, queen, worker and soldier termites. Soldier termites protect the rest of the colony and have large jaws that they use as weapons.

Soldier termite

Worker termite

Fantastic flies!

In winter, flies die from cold and hunger. Before they die, they lay eggs in sheltered places so that next year new flies will hatch.

Which insect can eat a house?

Termites can damage wooden houses by making their nests inside the wood. The damage cannot be seen from the outside until the wood is almost hollow. If anyone touches it, the house might collapse.

Which insect is a flying hunter?

Dragonflies are fierce flying hunters. Their huge eyes spot tiny prey such as midges and mayflies. They dash through the air and use their legs to catch their victims. Then they fly back to their perch to eat their meal.

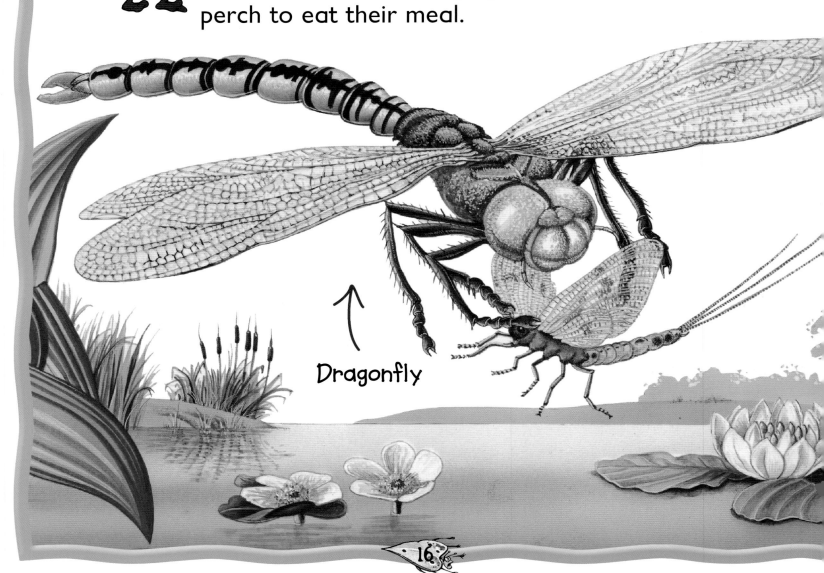

Dragonfly

Do insects like to pray?

The praying mantis is named because its front legs are folded, as if it is praying. In fact, it is waiting to grab some food. It waits for a fly or moth to come near, then SNAP! It grabs the victim very quickly with its front legs.

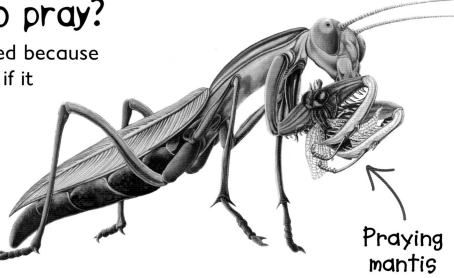

Praying mantis

Remember

Can you remember what dragonflies like to eat? Read these pages again to find out.

Can insects spread disease?

Many insects spread germs and disease. The mosquito is one of the deadliest. In hotter parts of the world, when it bites people to suck their blood, it may pass on a terrible illness such as malaria or yellow fever.

Playing dead!

When in danger, the click beetle falls onto its back and pretends to be dead. When the danger has gone, it arches its body and then straightens out with a jerk and a 'click'!

Why are scorpions' tails so deadly?

Scorpions have poisonous stings at the end of their tails. They use them to attack their victims. Scorpions may also wave their tails at enemies to warn them that, unless they go away, they will sting them to death!

Scorpion

Which beetle carries a spray gun?

The bombardier beetle squirts out a spray of smelly liquid from its rear end, almost like a small spray gun! This startles and stings an attacker and gives the beetle time to escape.

Discover

Spiders and scorpions belong to the same family group. Try and find out what the group is called.

Scary spiders!

The name 'tarantula' was first given to a type of wolf spider from Europe. Tarantulas are the biggest type of spider and live in hot parts of the world.

Black widow spider

What is the deadliest spider?

Black widow spiders are the most feared and dangerous of all spiders. They are small, shiny and black and they have a poisonous bite that can kill people. After mating, the female black widow spider may eat the male.

Why are there spiders in the bath?

Hornet

House spider

House spiders don't go in the bath to get clean. They hunt at night, and may slide into a bath by accident. The sides of the bath are too steep and slippery for them to climb out.

Hornet–moth

When is a hornet not a hornet?

The hornet-moth looks similar to a large type of wasp known as a hornet. This wasp has a very painful sting, but the hornet-moth is harmless. However, few other creatures dare to eat it as they think it is a wasp.

Grow up!

The American cicada is a kind of grasshopper. Its young live underground and they can take 17 years to change into adults!

Can ants join the army?

Ants don't really join the army. Army ants, travel in large groups of about 10,000 insects. They crawl in long lines through the forest, eating whatever they can bite and overpower, including spiders, lizards and birds.

Play

With a group of friends, get in a line and march around like a group of army ants.

Why do ladybirds have spots?

Ladybirds have bright pink, yellow or red bodies that are covered in black spots. These bright colours and spots tell other animals not to eat them, as they don't taste very nice.

Ladybird

Which insect glows at night?

Fireflies are not flies but a type of beetle. They produce a green or yellow light from their stomachs to attract a partner. Fireflies live on plants and trees during the day and are only active at night.

Firefly ➔

Think

Can you name any other insects or animals that have spots?

Sticking around!

Stick and leaf insects look exactly like sticks and leaves. When the wind blows, they rock and sway in the breeze like real twigs and leaves.

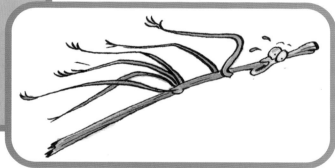

Can beetles dive?

Yes, beetles can dive. The great diving beetle lives in ponds and lakes and is a fast and fierce hunter. It uses its legs like paddles to dive through the water and catch its food.

Why do ants cut up leaves?

Leaf cutter ants cut up small sections of leaves to take back to their nests. The ants then carry the leaves back to a special 'ant' garden where they are stored and used as food for the ants.

Tough bug!

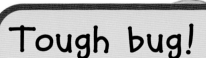

The young of the cranefly or 'daddy long-legs' is called a leather jacket after its tough skin.

Why do moths like the moonlight?

Most moths, such as the Indian moon moth, like moonlight. They use it to search for plant juices such as nectar in flowers. By day they rest in cracks in rocks or among leaves.

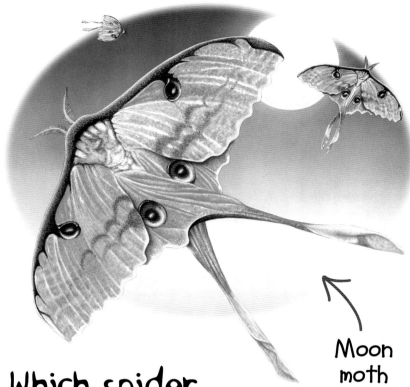

Moon moth

Which spider looks like a crab?

Crab spiders look like small crabs with wide bodies and curved legs. They sit on flowers and lie in wait for small insects to grab and eat.

Leafcutter ants

Think
Do you know of any other animals that become active after dark?

Which bug has the most legs?

Centipedes are long and thin, and usually have more than 30 legs. There are more than 3000 types of centipede. Millipedes are even longer and may have up to 100 legs.

Centipede

Millipede

Draw

Use brightly coloured pens or pencils and draw your very own crab spider.

What are the greediest insects?

Locusts are a type of grasshopper. They live in dry, warm places. If locusts find a field of crops, they swoop down in large swarms and begin to feast. The whole field can be gone in less than an hour.

Thorny tail

The thorn bug has a hard, pointed body that makes it look like a thorn on a plant.

Can spiders change colour?

Crab spiders hide themselves in flowers and plants so they can catch food. They change colour to match their surroundings so that other insects can't see them. This is called camouflage.

Gold leaf crab spider →

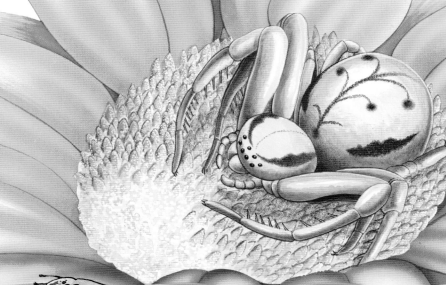

Do earwigs really live in ears?

Earwigs don't really crawl into ears or hide in wigs. But they do like dark, damp corners. At night they come out to feed on flower petals, one of their favourite foods.

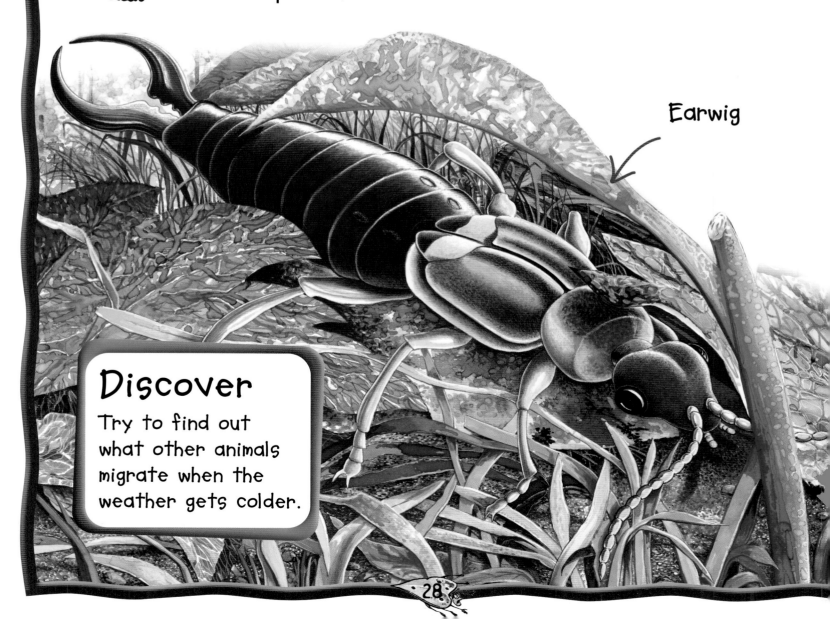

Earwig

Discover

Try to find out what other animals migrate when the weather gets colder.

How do insects help flowers to grow?

Many insects, including butterflies, visit flowers to collect nectar and pollen. They carry the pollen from flower to flower. This helps flowers form seeds or fruits so that new plants can grow.

Painted lady butterfly

Wonderful webs!

A web-spinning spider makes a new web almost every night – eating the old one to recycle (use again) the silk threads.

Where do insects spend winter?

Some insects travel to warmer lands when the weather gets cold. This is called migration. In North America, monarch butterflies fly south during autumn. They spend the winter in warmer parts of America and fly north again in the spring.

Quiz time

Do you remember what you have read about insects and spiders? These questions will test your memory. The pictures will help you. If you get stuck, read the pages again.

3. Can insects walk on water?

page 9

page 11

4. How many times can a bee sting you?

page 5

1. How many wings does an insect have?

page 12

5. Can spiders spit?

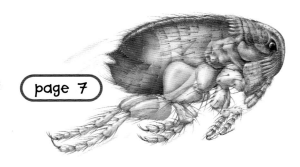

page 7

2. How far can a flea jump?

6. Do insects like to pray?

page 17

7. Can insects spread disease?

page 17

11. Why do moths like the moonlight?

page 25

8. Why are scorpions' tails so deadly?

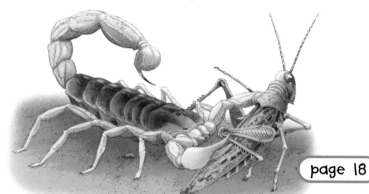

page 18

12. Which spider looks like a crab?

page 25

9. What is the deadliest spider?

page 19

13. Which bug has the most legs?

page 27

page 17
page 25
page 18
page 25
page 27
page 19
page 22

Answers

1. Two pairs of wings
2. Over 30 centimetres
3. Yes, the pondskater can
4. A bee can only sting once
5. Yes, the spitting spider can
6. The praying mantis folds its front legs as if it is praying
7. Yes, the mosquito can pass on malaria
8. Their tails have poisonous stings
9. The black widow spider
10. To tell other animals not to eat them
11. It helps them search for food
12. The crab spider
13. The millipede

10. Why do ladybirds have spots?

page 22

Index